THE ORACLE OF THE PROGRAMMER

YOU HAVE THE RIGHT TO BE LAZY

GUILLERMO CERCEAU

edited, translated and published by Caobo

BE 0723.947.028

Belgium, 2019

ISBN 9781688965812

first published in Spanish

by Ediciones Ocean Consulting C.A

Venezuela, 2003

All dictums and introductory text free for consultation on the website

https://caobo.org/oracle

For my brother, Fernando.

CONTENTS

ABOUT THE AUTHOR

Guillermo Cerceau (Argentina, 1957) is a consultant specialized in new technologies. He has worked for twenty years in the corporate world, first as an independent consultant and then, at KPMG, for almost 11 years, where he reached the position of CIO for Venezuela. Currently researching cities, migrations, climate change, and advanced technologies like AI, VR, AR and so-called «Smart Cities».

AUTHOR'S NOTE FOR THE ENGLISH TRANSLATION

This small book was written 20 years ago, between 1998 and 1999, while I was the CIO of a prominent consulting firm and published, in Spanish, in 2000. Its object was to help my staff when they got into "programmers block," and it was addressed to both coders and support personnel. In those days, programmers were more or less self-taught and very young, so I decided to use, as much as possible, references to pop and New Age culture, thinking that I could reach their souls better. But, with few exceptions, they didn't care for references, reading or anything besides tech stuff. Even if I find today the book a bit naïve, and without a doubt, old fashioned, I still believe the approach to the problems of creating software is valid. As I explain in the text, the general ideas were taken from Brian Eno's Oblique Strategies; in those days several "oracles" like the *I Ching* and the Runes were very popular among young people. I am grateful to Caobo Ediciones and to Tessa Debilde, who took the initiative to rescue this book from oblivion and went through the hard work of translating it.

PRELIMINARY NOTE

This Oracle has been written by a programmer for other programmers. It doesn't have any other ambition than to share reflections about the art of programming, in the spirit of those renaissance artisans Paolo Rossi mentions in his beautiful book 'Philosophy, Technology, and the Arts in the Early Modern Era'. The following passage from that book summarizes our ideals:

The men who worked in the workshops, at the dockyards, in the shops, or who, without distancing from their practices, regarded the acts that were performed there as a form of knowledge, started to theorize about labour and assigned it some distinct aims which were undoubtedly more personal than individual sanctity or literary immortality.

(translation by editor)

The reader will determine for him or herself in which way these reflections are useful to their work. The form of an 'oracle' aims to give a more fun dynamic to the reading than that of an essay and attempts, we hope, to serve as a helping hand during moments of 'lack of inspiration'.

I. INTRODUCTION

We have to make this machine work; to make it create the items that the user desires, to make those in the best way possible: easily, fast, without errors; and that the results that it produces are trustworthy and appropriate. That is to say, we have to program a computer. This task is carried out daily by tens of thousands of artisans all over the world.

The programmer of today may be a kind of artisan-proletarian, similar to the artisans of the end of the Middle Age: he's working on an assembly line like any other worker, each day more and more integrated in industrial-type structures (contrary to what one might believe reading the literature about the 'information society', in which the writers present idyllic scenes about the working life of the programmers), yet retains in a certain way the spirit of the independent artisan who aspires to achieve his Masterpiece.

Style, that 'vertical and lonely dimension of thoughts', as Barthes calls it in his famous book *Writing Degree Zero*, is disappearing from academic texts, from encyclopedias, from the language of journalists; wallowed up by the postmodernist uniformity. Strangely enough, it has found refuge in the work of programmers; because if in any fragment of nonliterary text the style becomes visible, it's in the source code of a computer program.

In this introduction, we reflect on specific subjects related to the job of programming. We also confess here an inbuilt deficiency of the aphorisms ahead. Many years ago I read a beautiful book on the art of writing short stories that stated more or less the following: 'the ideas I express here are useless because they will be incomprehensible to those who haven't had them themselves, and to all others, they will be unnecessary'. This warning does not declare the uselessness of this book but instead points out the paradoxical aspect of all teachings, and the difficulty of communicating the knowledge behind a practice.

The difficulty starts early: what is a machine? Who are the users? We operate with words like 'easy to use', 'efficient', to define their expectations, but what do these words actually mean? We continuously work with terms we barely understand but which, in a certain way, mark our course.

The computer, as a thing, as a device that you buy in a store, take out of a box, plug into the electricity and turn on using a button, is a machine. But it's a machine that serves absolutely no purpose, it's almost fictitious, like those perpetual motion machines that consumed the most fertile imaginations from the Renaissance until the 19th century. If this machine wants to do something useful, it needs a series of elements: the *software*, the operating systems, applications, the actions of the users, etc. Once those elements are present, we no longer have a machine but something we'll refer to as an 'informatic system'. I'm very aware that the phrase is unpleasant and that the terminology that composes it is problematic. A system is a term associated with joint disciplines (engineering, for example), with schools of philosophy, with specific thinkers (there is a

'Systems Theory') who probably wouldn't approve the use that it's been given here. Informatics and all its derivatives, on the other side, are the product of a particular way of viewing technology of information. But the sentence comes easily; it allows me to escape from the paradigm of the machine I don't believe in and saves me the extremely arduous work of inventing a satisfactory neologism.

An informatics system is not a machine; it can't be understood with the same conceptual tools that we use to understand machines, nor can it be programmed the same way machines are programmed. Similarly, a 'user' is not an innocent and interchangeable beneficiary of any given tool; there are no 'users' of hammers or televisions, of pans, bicycles, or hair combs. Why are there computer users? Who are these extraordinary beings, who need extensive and expensive training, and who are never happy? A computer user doesn't establish the same relationship with his 'machine' as a mason with his spade or a painter with his brush, a television viewer with his television or a driver with his car. This elementary point should lead us to think that the computer ('an informatic system') is a tool of a different nature than all other tools and that its use implies a distinct relationship with it than one could have with any other tools.

The purpose of this book is to examine those differences and from them explain the process of programming so that we can understand its most challenging obstacles. In particular, we focus on that which in art and literature is commonly referred to as 'creative block': those moments in which inspiration seems to abandon us, our talents are lost, and we find ourselves alone facing a problem that, in the strange irony life, is always urgent

Hence the 'oracle' format of this essay; the possibility to use it as a 'manual for consulting' similar to the *I Ching,* or the cards of Brian Eno. If we leave aside the superstitious or magical use often given to oracles, which have nothing to do with the metaphoric resonance we attempt here, any 'divination system' that humanity has conceived has as a primary purpose to help those that consult them make decisions; to escape the traps that our mind sets for us and to serve as a starting point for reflections that always go beyond the dictum of the oracle itself, same way a child plays to see figures of animals in the shapes of clouds or flames. But before we enter into the considerations of our oracle, we'd like to shed light over a conceptual base from which to read the rest of the essays, that, although independent from one another, are subject to the same principles. We want to examine some different views on the relation between the programmer or the user and the computer.

II. CONCEPTS

A NAIVE CONCEPT

In the mind of many programmers, and of the general public, there is a concept that we consider 'naive', which presents the work of the programmer as that of the technician who gives 'orders' to the machine. This naive way of thinking, in a certain way, is based on the relationship that users establish with their computers. They, effectively, give 'orders', to the programs they're using: 'open a file', 'print a document', 'save a file', correct the spelling of a text, solve a specific calculation. It seems as if the computer obeys those orders, executes the indicated tasks, and it's that practice of the user that creates the base of the paradigm:

orders ⟶ machine ⟶ results

On the other hand, this concept has been influenced by cybernetics since the 1940s, when the first computers were built. The programmers, in those days, were generally electrical engineers, scientists or mathematicians, and the machines of the time were just that, 'machines', devices more akin to a calculator than to a modern computer. Consequently, 'programming' meant establishing the physical connection between circuits. In that sense, it wasn't very different from creating the operating parameters for any machine in the assembly line of a factory, like those in the textile, metallurgic, or graphic industry. Several centuries of mechanistic thinking in sciences and in some areas of philosophy had given the engineers and scientists of the time a very dominant paradigm. Their 'ideology' continued to be transmitted in textbooks, reference books of informatics and of course, in popular consciousness.

A paradigm, according to Kuhn's definition, is unconscious, and it's no use to discuss with the users or even the programmers to prove that theirs is 'false'. In fact, it's not true or false, but rather an interpretative scheme, a 'base for thinking' about human practice. It doesn't change with words or mental exercises, as pretended by a variety of ill-informed consultants, because if that were true, it would challenge the very definition of a paradigm. We can, however, modify perception, attitudes, or valorization about inevitable operational consequences of a paradigm. If paradigms were consciously accessible for individuals, they would cease to be paradigms and become objects of thought. These objects can be weighed against another paradigm, but the latter only changes when people's practice change. A computer operator who transcribes texts in a word processor isn't giving his computer any orders; he's interacting with it. As interfaces (the 'software' elements between the user and the computer) become more complex and easier to use, as programs 'learn' from their users and begin to execute tasks without needing an explicit command, the user will modify his view on his relationship with the computer as well. Just look at how we use automatic dictionaries and search engines now.

In the case of programmers, it's much harder, because the interaction between them and an informatics system is much more complex, and a large part of the tasks they perform looks a lot like orders. Many of the old programming languages and almost all operating systems talk about 'commands', 'instructions' and 'tasks', each of which results in the machine executing specific actions. With the appearance of the new 'non procedural' languages, object-oriented programming', those languages not based on commands, interfaces and graphic operating systems, and languages such as HTML and others (variants of the SGML), which are languages that define the 'what' and not the 'how' of what we want of the system; all of these new technologies (and others that we can barely catch a glimpse of), will slowly cut loose the programmers from the old paradigms.

Far beyond the inadequacy of this naive vision, are the consequences it has on the expectation of the user about what the programmer can do, how much time it takes him and how satisfactory the results are. This is because this paradigm supposes, like in the case of the first engineers, that the programmer exactly knows what he wants the computer to do, like any engineer who 'programs' an industrial machine to perform specific tasks has to know precisely the diameter of the nuts and bolts the machine should make, or like the rabbi who knew precisely what he wanted the *Golem* to do.

A MORE REALISTIC CONCEPT

A more advanced paradigm is the one that conceives the relation between programmer and computer as a dialogue: it's no longer about a master giving orders to a slave (a *Golem*), but rather about two entities, one human and the other artificial, who engage in a cooperative dialogue to realize a task, in our case, the task of writing a program for the users. We represent that situation as follows:

programmer ⟶ computer

computer ⟶ programmer

Here, the user still supposes that the programmer is almost all-knowing, only that now he believes the 'machine' is no longer passive, like other machines, and that it can help out in certain things. The user's expectations remain the same, as well as the results that programmers deliver.

THE COMPLETE CONCEPT

But the new software tools, together with the technological and social transformations that are taking place now, make this paradigm as well inadequate to understand the true nature of the relationship between the programmer, the user, and the informatics system. It is a complete relationship, circular, which goes much further than giving orders to a machine (if that expression makes sense) or to establish a dialogue with it. It's a complex loop (as Edgar Morin would mean), which we can represent as follows:

operator

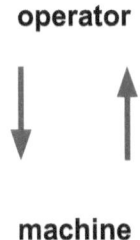

machine

The programmer changes his concept of what should be done all throughout his interrelation with the system, which he modifies to respond to this new consciousness; the modified system reacts to the programmer, proposing a new vision of the system that is unraveling, and this circular relationship goes through these loops as many times as necessary to elaborate the expected result.

How far we are from the omnipotent engineer, the cabalist that gives precise orders to an inert, obedient, and dead machine! How far we are from the human who precisely knows what to ask of an artificial system and who can communicate with it!

The programmer can't know beforehand what the end product of his work will be. He never really knew it: the new paradigm helps him to understand why he never knew it and never will know it. Further ahead, in the dictums, we tackle the cognitive and organizational aspects derived from the complete concept, which we do in the form of the oracle, trying to open up more questions than to establish definitive answers.

III. BEHIND THE ORACLE

Now that we have established this initial framework, we'll address the oracle. This pamphlet, in its essence, has nothing original to it. The basic idea comes out of the use of the card deck by Brian Eno, one of the fascinating musicians of the nineties, who created a card game to use in case of 'creative block'. Eno's cards come with instructions to help the musician in his work:

■ Honour thy error as a hidden intention
■ Try faking it
■ Use an old idea
■ Do something boring
■ Only one element of each kind
■ State the problem in words as clearly as possible and many others in the same tone.

Eno, on top of being a musician, producer, and creator of digital art, is an artist closely in touch with the technological avant-garde in North America, and his reflections notably influenced some of the creators of new technology, above all related to the internet. He was a pioneer in the use of personal computers to create music and visual art, and his web presence is broad enough to find him while surfing about various subjects of a different nature, which shows his ample interests and influence.

On the other hand, (and take note that I'm an atheist, foreign to all superstition) the use of oracles to make decisions is as antique as civilization. The *I Ching*, reputed as one of the oldest books of humanity, is the most known. The Tarot, reading the flight of birds, interpreting the shapes of the clouds or the entrails of a sacrificed animal, are as well expressions of this activity of 'giving meaning' which characterizes us as humans.

These references to the *I Ching* and Brian Eno aren't as alien to computers and programming as one might think at first sight. The German mathematician Leibniz knew about the ancient Chinese oracle thanks to his relationship with Jesuit explorers, who were since the 16th century the ideological avant-garde of the European empires' expansion into Asia. It is said that Leibniz invented (or discovered) the binary number system contemplating the hexagrams or drawings of 6 lines that make up the *I Ching*. As it happens, Leibniz is one of the fathers of the two fundamental elements of modern computer science: the invention of one of the first mechanical calculators, and the start of what later would be called symbolic logic (aside from the binary numbers mentioned earlier).

By emulation, perhaps out of laziness, I partially copied the scheme of *I Ching*. Each subject has his own 'dictum', his 'explanation', (which would be equivalent to the 'images'), and its commentaries, like those supposedly written by Confucius as an appendix to each hexagram. Not to fall into an anachronism, which sooner or later would be discovered, the comments in this book are obviously not from Confucius, but from various other characters: musicians, architects, philosophers, mathematicians. I could have used classic authors from our art, like Wirth, Ritchie, or Knuth (I did use some of them). But I preferred poets, musicians, mystics, philosophers, for two reasons. First, the books of earlier mentioned and cited authors, although masterpieces and often landmarks in the history of computing are, I believe, difficult to read for the majority of today's programmers. Second, by citing texts of other artisans we hope to reinforce the underlying idea behind the aphorisms, that our art is an art like any other and has the same advantages and disadvantages, problems and happiness of any other art form.

Ultimately, it's about what man makes; his praxis, about that production-reproduction of the world of which Hegel and his disciples talk. To program a computer is, in a small way, to modify the world; a poem from Borges may help us see this clearly.

At about three or four hundred meters
of the Pyramid I bent down, took a handful
of sand, and dropped it silently a little
further and I said in a low voice: I'm modifying
the Sahara. The act was minimal, but the simple
words were accurate and I thought
all my life had been necessary for me to
say them.

Jorge Luis Borges
(translation by editor)

If the eventual consultation of this oracle serves to unblock some programmer in one of those unfortunate moments where he must deliver a program or a routine in ten minutes, and has no idea where to start, I'll feel satisfied. Surely I won't find out if it happens, but that is only a *bug* of the oracle which, for reasons of coherence, I refuse to eliminate.

IV. HOW TO CONSULT THE ORACLE

This book can be read in sequence, like a book instead of an oracle, as a collection of small essays of a fragmentary nature about the art of programming.

But it can also be used as a consultation book, for those moments in which, as happens to any creator, inspiration doesn't arrive, we're stuck in a dead-end, or we simply don't know how to continue. Ultimately, an oracle is a tool to assist decision-making.

You might think that using an oracle to make important life decisions is irrational because it entrusts blind chance with decisions that should be subject to rational considerations. But, what does it mean to make a rational analysis of a situation? In reason's own terms, this task is a practical impossibility. Except in extremely trivial situations, any decision requires knowledge of an immense amount of variables, often hard or impossible to take into account adequately, even more so to measure their reciprocal influences.

An example: if we doubt in the morning when we leave the house whether to bring the umbrella or not, we won't find the answer in a set of differential equations and carefully gathered values measured in different parts of the globe. Most likely we'll just look at the sky and think: today it will rain, or maybe we'll toss a coin, or take the umbrella without thinking too much about it. In any case, the 'rationality' of our decision isn't in our method, but in the non-learned certainty that whatever we do, it will or will not rain according to the will of the sky, which is (without instant access to data from satellites and supercomputers) inscrutable.

The oracle is nothing more (but nothing less) than a formalization of this unconscious mental process through which we make millions of decisions each day. If we use chance as an instrument to access an answer, the ambiguity of it puts the decisions in our own hands, and the only thing we obtain is a mental truce.

To consult the oracle:

1. You'll need a coin, pen, and paper.

Assign value 1 (one) to one side of the coin and value 0 (zero) to the other side. In principle, it doesn't matter which side of the coin is assigned which value; still, if we follow the tradition of the *I Ching* and give the process a more mystic tone, we recommend value 1 (or the positive value) for heads, and value 0 (or negative), for tails.

2. Think about the question you want the oracle to answer.

3. Toss the coin five times.

Note down the result each time, according to instruction 1, and then proceed from right to left. For example, if we determined that heads [H] equals 1 and tails [T] equals 0, after five tosses, we could have the following result:

H H T H T

We construct a binary number:

1 1 0 1 0

which, as we can determine by simple conversion (or, in case of a very lazy reader, by looking at the conversion table), corresponds to decimal number 26.

4. Find the binary number in the list...

...or the oracle corresponding to number 26 and read the dictum (what the oracle advises you to do), the explanation (the meaning of the oracle) and the comments, generally a text of a well-known author, which serve as a kind of *hypertext*, to circulate from one aphorism to another. Not all oracles have this last section.

Another method, used with the *I Ching*, the Bible, or any text sufficiently complex, is to select a dictum randomly. This method, although often used, isn't recommended, because of the natural tendency of humans to avoid extremes and to open a book always more or less in the center, thus eliminating many options that the coin method, thanks to the generosity and neutrality of chance, takes into account.

In any case, this pamphlet doesn't possess more magic than the reader attributes to it and possibly serves as something fun. Someone might even find useful or pleasant lessons in it.

DECIMAL: BINARY

0: «0 0 0 0 0. Understanding»

1: «0 0 0 0 1. New tools»

2: «0 0 0 1 0. When does it end?»

3: «0 0 0 1 1. Deadline»

4: «0 0 1 0 0. Magic»

5: «0 0 1 0 1. It's not a machine»

6: «0 0 1 1 0. The user»

7: «0 0 1 1 1. Where to look for help?»

8: «0 1 0 0 0. Bugs»

9: «0 1 0 0 1. Between the client and the user»

10: «0 1 0 1 0. Reinvent the wheel»

11: «0 1 0 1 1. Style and programming»

12: «0 1 1 0 0. Follow the diagram»

13: «0 1 1 0 1. You have the right to be lazy»

14: «0 1 1 1 0. The temporary and the definitive»

15: «0 1 1 1 1. Discipline»

16: «1 0 0 0 0. Start over»

17: «1 0 0 0 1. Distractions»

18: «1 0 0 1 0. You're each time further away»

19: «1 0 0 1 1. Your world doesn't belong to you»

20: «1 0 1 0 0. Irresponsibility»

21: «1 0 1 0 1. Inexpressible»

22: «1 0 1 1 0. Yesterday it worked fine»

23: «1 0 1 1 1. The program keeps on running in your head»

24: «1 1 0 0 0. The blind spot»

25: «1 1 0 0 1. Worlds within worlds»

26: «1 1 0 1 0. Objects without objects»

27: «1 1 0 1 1. Close your eyes and try to see»

28: «1 1 1 0 0. False solutions»

29: «1 1 1 0 1. The simplest solution»

30: «1 1 1 1 0. Don't do anything»

31: «1 1 1 1 1. The masterpiece»

0 0 0 0 0. UNDERSTANDING

One never understands things, one just gets used to
them.

EXPLANATION

Don't worry about understanding, that imperative that we have imposed ourselves without anybody asking us to; which consumes our nights, prevents us from finding the solutions which, from their obviousness, scream for our attention, while we submerge ourselves deaf in the useless ocean of comprehension: you never understand things, you get used to them. Those who believe they understand a problem or its solution simply confuse understanding with familiarity.

Understanding is a state of the soul that doesn't belong to the manipulation of formal systems; it has to do with experience, with life.

Epistemological model

Here you have

a big box

labeled

box

When you open it,

you find inside

a box

labeled

box

from a box

labeled

box.

When you open it –

I mean this

box now,

not that one –

you find inside

a box

labeled

and so on,

and when you

go on in this way,

you find

after infinite efforts

an infinite small

box

with so small

a label,

that it evaporates,

as it were.

before you eyes.

It is a box

that only exists in your

imagination.

A perfectly empty

box.

'Epistemological Model'

H. Magnus Ensenzberger in: Shea, Christopher Giuggio, "The Wreck

of Titanic: A Comedy" (2014). Senior Projects Spring 2014. Paper 15.

http://digitalcommons.bard.edu/senproj_s2014/15

0 0 0 0 1. NEW TOOLS

Don't change tools (or versions), unless the new features are beneficial to your project. In any case, don't cultivate false hope.

EXPLANATION

Well, you've 'updated' your tools: now you've got version x.z instead of x.0. Admittedly this version has new capacities, new features, that will make -so you think- your life as an artisan easier. Except in those cases, very common in Windows-based products, when this new 'version' simply corrects some defect (it's not a 'new' version, but the same old product, now fixed), the new features are just a mirage. Sooner or later you will understand that your work is the same and that new possibilities will, in turn, have their own difficulties.

Complexity can not be exorcised. If you remove it from one point of the program, it appears in another. It's like the -1 in math.

There is the anecdote of a senior executive on holiday who meets a fisherman. While contemplating the beauty of the tropical paradise they're in; they begin a conversation. "Have you thought," the executive asks the fisherman "about buying a boat, and thus fish more?". The fisherman answers him that he has enough to live on with what he catches. The executive insists: "But if you'd have a boat, you could increase your production, sell what you don't consume and save up money to buy more boats…" The fisherman asks again: "Why would I want to buy so many boats?" The executive answers: "Because this way, you'd make a lot of money, you could have a lot of time off and do like me, I take vacations and come here to fish." The fisherman answers: "But I'm already here fishing!"

Of course, the irony is that he's wrong. The executive can stop fishing anytime he wants, the fisherman will have to do it all the time, with little possibility to change his way of life. But in one way, it illustrates the fact that certain evolutions reach their starting point on a higher level.

Certain phenomena evolve through time like fractals: if we observe them during a long enough period, we see that the whole reproduces in the parts. When we take that same observation from inside the phenomenon, this presents itself to us with a certain circularity.

If we see what's happened with the generation of visual tools and programming languages (C++, Visual Basic, Java) we find ourselves almost back at the start, when we could only count on the assembler, Basic, or Pascal.

0 0 0 1 0. WHEN DOES IT END?

A program is never finished.

EXPLANATION

Your program is ready, documentation, and *help* included. Well, the program is ready, the documentation and the *help* will be ready in a few days. In any case, the user can already have it in his hands. Is it really what the client requested? Perhaps. Is it what they needed? Probably. Will it work without errors? No. To deliver a finished product, if such a thing ever happens in programming, is to be caught between these four cardinal points: the need of the customer, the perception he or she has of his or her own needs (philosophically one could argue that they're the same thing, when you have to charge your fees, you'll discover they're not), your understanding of this perception and the practical result of that understanding. You'll find one day, by accident (a casual visit to your client perhaps), that the accounting tool that took you so much work, is used ceremoniously by the client, who enters the data according to your precise instructions and pays you for 'maintenance', but that the results presented to his bosses come from a spreadsheet, constructed by an anonymous accounting assistant in a hidden corner of the administration. Don't despair: your products are expensive, they provide you with a dignified life, but they're absolutely useless.

Perhaps there aren't words more appropriate to conclude this explanation than that medieval aphorism reincarnated in T.S Elliot' Four Quartets: "*In my end is my beginning.*"

COMMENTS

Any program, when it works, is already obsolete.

(Murphy's law, adapted to computers)

0 0 0 1 1. DEADLINE

Every deadline was calculated, underestimating the
complexity of the problem. It is necessary to negotiate new
dates with the client.

EXPLANATION

We've known for decades, and there's enough literature on the matter, that no computer project ends on the agreed date. The administration of projects is an engineering discipline invented so that this disparity between the planned and the reality is not excessive; but, even with the best project manager, yours won't end on the scheduled day. The reasons are plenty: among others, there is our lack of understanding of formal systems and the disparity between what is wanted and what we believe is wanted.

Be pessimistic about schedules; exaggerate the time required for each task. Even so, you will fail, but you will have distinct possibilities to make friends with the project manager. Finally, make sure this last one doesn't know anything about your art.

0 0 1 0 0. MAGIC

No one forces you to do magic all the time. Do it only in your free time and only to feed your spirit.

The story of The Golem *stands as an example of how things we accomplish through magic sooner or later turn against us, just like happens to Mickey Mouse when he enchants the broom. As it has always been the case for artisans, you are at the service of a community of users. You must realize your* work, *and they must benefit from it.*

EXPLANATION

Years ago I heard the story of the *Golem*, from a rabbi in New England as it can be read in the books of Gershom Sholem and other Hebraists. It's a story that every programmer should know:

In the sixteenth century, the Rabbi of Prague, Judah Loew, during one of the many *pogroms* that the city suffered at the hands of Christians, uses magic to create a being of clay, as God does in the Book of Genesis. He writes a sentence on the forehead of the homunculus or feeds him a roll of paper with a phrase, depending on the version of the story. The *Golem* comes to life and destroys the enemies of the Jews. But, as it happens in science-fiction stories, something goes wrong, and the *Golem* begins to kill those he's supposed to protect. The rabbi, a great sage, changes the phrase he had inscribed on the *Golem*'s forehead (or, perhaps gives him a new roll to eat), and the *Golem* again becomes mud and loses his life.

This story has called the attention of computer scientists because, in no small extent, it is a parable about what computers are today: artificial beings, without life, to whom we feed a text called a program, and they carry out an activity to our advantage (by the way, computers were invented to kill people, during the Second World War, just like the *Golem*).

Now, suddenly, something is wrong; the monster doesn't exactly do what we tell it to do. It has a bug, and we have to correct it, 'do some maintenance' or replace it. We rarely have to resort to the Rabbi's solution of changing the software to destroy it, although this can also be done. In one version of the legend, the Rabbi only has to change one letter of the text that gave life to the *Golem*, and it's enough to destroy it.

Many times the programmer is expected to perform magic, like his mystic predecessor. After all, his skills look like magic when he solves issues that analysts find inconceivable. The difference between the modern programmer and the old Hebrew saint is that the latter was recognized for his magic, and it was accepted that it came from God and obtained by the greatness of his spirit, while in the case of our programmer it's assumed that magic is part of his work, for which he's paid, and which has nothing supernatural about it. Big mistake: the programmer's magic is a product of his inspiration, which as the Greeks already knew, is of divine origin, and rather than part of his work, is an exceptional skill that he has cultivated thanks to the greatness of his spirit, just like the rabbi. Magic or divine inspiration isn't part of the work, and you can't pay for them: this is the very grave sin of simony, derived from Simon, the Magician who wanted to buy powers from the Apostle.

COMMENTS

In 1985, when National Public Radio reporter and witch Margot Adler was revising Drawing Down the Moon, her great social history of American Paganism, she surveyed the Pagan community and discovered that an 'amazingly' high percentage of folks drew their paychecks from technical fields and from the computer industry. Respondents gave many reasons for this curious affinity – everything from 'computers are elementals in disguise' to the simple fact that the computer industry provided jobs for the kind of smart, iconoclastic, and experimental folk that Paganism attracts. Pagans like to do things – to make mead, to publish zines, to wield swords during gatherings of the Society for Creative Anachronism. And many like to hack code.

Erik Davies, Technognosis, 1998 (https://techgnosis.com/technopagans/)

0 0 1 0 1. IT'S NOT A MACHINE

Do not always expect from your device, your operating system, your compiler or the application that you're building, the same 'fidelity' of a machine: its predictable behavior, its operational transparency, its nudity of an artifact made of parts. The strange behavior of your hardware or your software aren't anomalies that could be avoided or incomprehensible errors: they are part of its essence.

EXPLANATION

One can not apply the traditional idea of what a machine is to an entity as complex as what, for lack of a better word, we have called an informatic system: the set of devices and electronics, mechanical and symbolic systems that make up a computer and the programs that give it life. If we insist so much on this idea, it's because we're convinced that the perception of programmers and users, based on the paradigm of the machine, is largely responsible for many of the problems related to programming and the use of computers. Let's see why.

The currently prevailing mechanistic vision divides the world sharply between natural beings and artificial objects. In the last couple of decades, this view has entered into crisis. Computers would belong to the 'artificial' domain since they are quite clearly not produced by nature, but by man. If this division were one of those many semantic maps that we build to make sense of reality, it wouldn't cause significant inconveniences. The problem arises when these nomenclatures impose certain premises, which aren't even conscious. We expect certain things from natural beings and very different things from artificial objects. Maybe a few decades ago, these expectations were more or less correct; today they're not. Technology is producing objects, which indeed are 'artifacts' (made with art, etymologically), which aren't comparable to what we traditionally know as a machine. The behavior of a tractor or a blender is determined by the parts that compose them and the relations between these parts. The behavior of a computer, with its corresponding operating system, graphic interfaces, and set of applications, can be quite unpredictable. It depends vastly on the will of the programmer or the person who uses it. A great deal of headache for clients, users and creators alike results from understanding devices of the information technology as 'machines', when in fact, they are objects that don't respond to the old paradigm of nature versus artifacts. This paradigm defines the expectations and introduces actions that aren't always possible to satisfy or carry out. To continue assuming it as appropriate is to insist on generating frustration.

What is then, this *hardware-software* complex we call computers? They are new devices that we can only explain in terms of the technologies of the past through analogies. Yes, they're not natural beings, and much less intelligent or alive, as some recklessly suggest. It may not be elegant to say that they are halfway between these two extremes. Maybe it would be better to invent a new realm to place them: the realm of computers.

COMMENTS

They [the scientists preceding Newton, Bacon, and Descartes] have based their ideas on the mathematical theory of Isaac Newton, the philosophy of Rene Descartes, and the scientific methodology advocated by Francis Bacon, and developed them in accordance with the general conception of reality prevalent during the seventeenth, eighteenth, and nineteenth centuries. Matter was thought to be the basis of all existence, and the material world was seen as a multitude of separate objects assembled into a huge machine. Like human-made machines, the cosmic machine was thought to consist of elementary parts. Consequently, it was believed that complex phenomena could always be understood by reducing them to their basic building blocks and by looking for the mechanisms through which these interacted.

The Turning Point, F. Capra, 1992 (http://www.juwing.sp.ru/Capra/ CONTENTS.htm)

0 0 1 1 0. THE USER

The user will never be satisfied with the result of your work.

EXPLANATION

The computer user isn't like the user of any other machine, for example; the user who drives a tractor, or who uses a telephone or a hammer.

Machines, in general, have a reduced set of behaviors, a shortlist of responses they give to the user, of 'things they do'. Computers, on the other hand, do absolutely nothing, or maybe we could say, they can do anything. Both statements are true simultaneously, although in different ways.

They don't do anything: they don't move things, they don't alter the environment, etc.

They do anything: what they 'do', that is, manipulate symbols, they can do in a myriad of ways: drawing, writing, playing music, etc.

COMMENTS

Science News (February 16th, 1991, pg. 104, (https://www.sciencenews.org/archive/finding-fault) talks about a book by Ivars Peterson. "Computer programs are among the most complex products designed by humanity." confirms David Parnas, from Queens University of Ontario, and he adds: "they are also the least trustworthy." He continues: "These two factors (complexity, propensity to errors) are clearly related. Software errors are not caused by any fundamental flaw in our knowledge. In principle, we know everything there is to know about each instruction that is going to be executed. Software errors are caused by our inability to fully understand these complex products."

0 0 1 1 1. WHERE TO LOOK FOR HELP?

Look for help where it makes sense to look for it: where you can find it.

EXPLANATION

When we encounter a problem that we can't solve, we go to the programming manuals, to the 'help' function provided by the manufacturer or to a colleague who works with tools similar to ours. There is, however, a vast world of scientific literature, among which stand out the journals of the ACM, IEEE and many others, published by professional or scientific societies, that deal with so-called 'Computer Science'. Why not delve into it?

Since a few years, we can follow discussions in academic journals, international meetings, and places like Internet forums, about the relationship between academic production and practitioners. It is well known and a reason for reflection and concern, that very little of what the great theoretician produce reaches the programmer directly. The benefit of academic research reflects in better compilers or operating systems, in new paradigms of analysis or program design. But between the academic formulation of these products and their practical use stands the industry, which encapsulates this knowledge in concrete commodities, for example, a new compiler, faster, more efficient or with a better interface. Most of the work of 'computer scientists' (to the extent that we can read about it with some precision in specialized journals) is related to topics much too abstract to be useful to the programmer, and even to the computer industry itself. A typical example of this is the inversion of programs, the discipline that consists of producing the 'input' of a program from its 'output'. The subject is undoubtedly fascinating (and it is wonderfully treated by David Gries in his 'Science of Programming'), but, it lacks any practical utility for the programmer who has to build an inventory or an e-mail system.

The best place a programmer can go to for help remains the programmers' guild. You can consult a colleague on another continent; you can participate in discussion forums, which the manufacturers sometimes offer themselves, etc. These are just some items of the endless list of possibilities that the web provides. Recognize that you're part of an extensive community of people who are solving problems. Connect with them, ask for help, and give support.

0 1 0 0 0. BUGS

'Every non-trivial system has at least one error.' says a
traditional computer aphorism.

(A slightly modified version of this text first appeared in Internet World,
March 2001)

EXPLANATION

Edsger W. Dijkstra, one of the great thinkers and father of structured programming once said: "If debugging is the process of removing software
bugs, then programming must be the process of putting them in.". Half
of the books on programming talk about avoiding bugs and programming without errors; throughout the development of computation, various
methodologies have been created to prevent mistakes, and there is a
whole collection of classics dedicated to the subject.

But it is a fact that every non-trivial program, and many really trivial ones,
are affected by mistakes. Many times these mistakes are so subtle that
they only manifest in particular conditions, in such a way that a program

can be in use for several years, have gained the trust of the users, and, suddenly, fail in an operation in which it had never failed before. A particular combination of data, a changing situation in the environment, or any other factor that usually costs a lot to discover, make the error manifest.

Other times things are not so mysterious. The programs are simply handed over to the user without being thoroughly tested. The 'installation' process becomes a covert debugging, and the client a true 'guinea pig'. Those are the famous 'beta versions' that programmers deliver as if they were a finished product.

Why do these situations occur? To say that programmers are human and as such, make mistakes is an unobjectionable truth that explains nothing at all. Human beings also make TVs and smartphones, and yet it's almost impossible for those new devices to 'have errors' in operation. The rare times this happens, the provider repairs or replaces the product, and it practically never constitutes a traumatic event. In any case, the company that sold the defective device immediately claims its warranty from the manufacturer, who then makes every effort to ensure that the defect does not recur. In general, in appliances, in automobiles or any new merchandise, the 'errors' are not tolerated by the customer.

But errors in *software* are different. The user isn't only used to them, but even expects them, is tolerant of them, and only loses his patience when the error prevents him from operating. Why that difference? First, because as we have said, a computer system is not a machine, it is not an appliance anymore, and its level of complexity is infinitely more significant than that of a blender or even a car, with its thousands of parts and dozens of subsystems. The complexity is not in the number of components but in the relationship between them.

On the other hand, as we have also observed, computer users have a different character than the 'user' of other artifacts, meaning their expectations are different, as well as their reactions to incorrect or unexpected results.

Why are programs full of errors? If we leave aside clumsiness, ineptitude or professional incapacity, which are only responsible for a minority of the errors of a program, we come across another one of the paradoxes of this craft, to which our dictum refers: all programs, without exception, contain at least one error.

Errors are to a system, what stains are to leather or grain is to wood: they are marks of its authenticity, its identification as a unique object. The errors are consubstantial with programs: a program without errors possibly wouldn't work. This statement does not pretend to be a joke or irony: it is a conviction acquired throughout decades of programming.

If I am allowed an analogy with literary texts or with verbal discourses, we could affirm that there is no discourse without a lapsus or a perfect text in which we can't discover an inconsistency, on the semantic, lexical or syntactic level. We humans, when we express ourselves verbally or in writing, can't avoid introducing this type of 'errors' in what we say or write. In the sixties the linguists, especially the French, studied these imbalances of discourse, these faults (in the geological sense) that cross through each text and that, far from being part of an 'error' of the author, rather constitute the mark that reveals a meaning or even its aesthetic secret (in the case of literary texts).

We know that the source code of a program is not a literary text, nor are the programming languages equivalent to natural languages. But the human act of inscribing a text, the set of gestures and mental dispositions that make a concept manifest in a chain of symbols, is the same in both cases, regardless of the final form, its use, and its essence. And it is precisely this symbolization of mental representations that is full of geological faults, difficult sites, unexplored or little known corners. When this imaginary topography becomes symbols, when the programmer constructs his source text, he can not prevent these topological accidents of his inner world from coming along the beautiful hills and the carefully constructed buildings.

Why would a program of some complexity be impossible without any errors? Because it would mean that the whole process of the symbolization of representations has been radically transformed, which is not possible, man being the kind of creature he is.

COMMENTS

Thomas Stewart, in his book, states that it is practically impossible to build a complex software system without errors. He adds that 10% of the code takes care of all the program is supposed to do, and the other 90% takes care of finding mistakes, catching them, and making sure that they do not affect the crucial 10% that is really doing the work. (paraphrased from Fortune, July 10th, 1995, pg. 119)

0 1 0 0 1. BETWEEN THE CLIENT AND THE USER

Don't get caught in the dilemmas of the conflict
between the user and the client.

EXPLANATION

The programmer lives trapped in a dilemma that is rarely made explicit, which prevents him from escaping it. On the one hand, your client (usually a company or a department), asks you to create a program. In the case of business programs, it is generally about controlling some aspect of the company: its assets, its human resources, its finances. Ultimately, this means controlling the people who perform the functions.

On the other hand, users who may or may not be the same persons that we're calling 'the client', want the program to make their life easier. They want it to be simple, easy to use, 'friendly', they want it to do this or that, and usually most similar to how they are used to doing it manually.

The programmer's dilemma is to find a compromise between these two demands that can become contradictory or exclusive. If the company wants to control their income, how to make life easier for the user of the billing system? Our program will make it more difficult!

This dilemma must be exposed at the beginning of the work, taking into account the following considerations:

01. The purpose of the product is to provide the client (the company, the department,...) reliable, on time and accurate information, as far as the conditions of the operating environment of the system allow. If these objectives can be met while making life easier for the user (user-friendly, etc.), so much better. But that is not your goal. It might be a side effect.

02. When it's necessary to choose between the 'performance' (its response speed, its friendliness to the user, the versatility of its operations) and the previous objective, the latter must come first. In other words: we will always sacrifice 'performance' for control. A good programmer seeks the highest possible efficiency without deviating from the central objective of the project.

We frame all these considerations in the idea that programming is a craft at the service of a community of users, which includes customers and operators, working in a capitalist society with criteria of value based on profit. It doesn't matter how many kilometers of cheap rhetorics the consultants use on *empowerment*, Total Quality or similar things. Companies want to increase their profits, and computers were designed for that purpose.

In a different society, these considerations might seem inappropriate or even cruel. In these notes, they are only realistic.

0 1 0 1 0. REINVENT THE WHEEL

Don't despair when you feel you're reinventing the wheel: if you check your conscience, you will find that, except when you're in a hurry, you enjoy it. Many times it's easier to reinvent your wheel than trying to use someone else's.

EXPLANATION

Every dedicated programmer, sooner or later, rediscovers the same fundamental concepts, the tricks of the experts. From subroutines, that initial discovery that we all made in our early Basic or *assembler* programs, before knowing that there is a unique construct in the language for it (macros in the case of the assembler), to the convenient possibility of 'hiding' the variables and procedures of a specific part of a program, before even hearing of object-oriented programming. This process doesn't mean the programmer should ignore the advances in the science of programming; it's just that he shouldn't feel any inferiority complex reading some journals that may be as illegible to him as Latin was for the fifteenth-century artisans.

COMMENTS

The French potter Bernard Palissy, quoted by Paolo Rossi in 'Philosophy, Technology, and the Arts in the Early Modern Era', wrote in 1580: "Is it possible for a man to know something and be aware of the natural effects without having read the books written in Latin by the philosophers?" Rossi tells us that Palissy was one of those craftsmen who theorize about his practice.

0 1 0 1 1. STYLE AND PROGRAMMING

*Get acquainted with the canon of programming norms
very well; the manuals generally establish guidelines for the
name of variables and procedures, indentation mode, and
other stylistic aspects. Memorize them and then work to
forget them.*

EXPLANATION

Is there anything such as 'pure detonation'? Is that nightmare, disguised as a dream of the logicians of the turn of the century, and the few logical positivists still active today, true? Was it ever true? Of course not. Any mathematician knows how the shape of symbols influences their ability to think of a theorem or solution to an equation. Among other reasons, it was his superior symbolism that gave Leibnitz preeminence over Newton in integral calculus, even though both men discovered (or invented) this branch of mathematics almost simultaneously. In some ways, the $\int$ of the

Leibnizian integral rule and the symbology of his derivatives were more favorable to mathematicians than the fluxions of Newton.

Definitely yes, the elements of formal languages contain connotations. A specific 'style' manifests itself in the source code of the programmers.

How could the result not reflect these non-explicit elements of a program? How can we manage that 'intangible' part of an intangible thing that is software? What methodology could put an order in that 'vertical and solitary dimension of thought'? In the same way source code is text (and that's what it is, in all its rights), it's subject to the unconscious laws that govern the production of any text as well.

The final result, the program we aimed for, doesn't depend entirely on these denotative and stylistic elements if it did they would be unpredictable and enigmatic artifacts: they would be works of art. But it would be a significant error of appreciation to assume that this aspect of programming has nothing to do with the obtained result with the administration of programming projects, and with the so-called 'software crisis', which as we have already said, doesn't only end with each new methodology that announces his death, but it also presents us with new fronts.

COMMENTS

Donald Knuth makes the following statement, in his book Literate Programing.

"Programming can be considered as the process of creating literary works, intended to be read. The literature of the 'program genre' is to be executed by machines, but that is not its primary purpose. A computer program that is beautiful, useful, and profitable, should be able to be read by human beings.»

0 1 1 0 0. FOLLOW THE DIAGRAM

Follow the instructions of the analyst, captured in the diagram (flow, structure, objects) and let your imagination fill in what is missing. No diagram can ever capture the intention of a man.

EXPLANATION

"What is now proved was once, only imagined," wrote William Blake in number 33 of his 'Proverbs of Hell'. We could paraphrase it as follows: what is now built or programmed, was first purely *imagined*. The things that man does exist because he first imagines them; because, in some mysterious way, they exist first in his mind. But in his mind they can not exist in the same way as in the 'world': in the mind, there is nor time nor extension, things have absolute flexibility, which is rare in the real world, where things are material, have weight, opacity... That's the reason why Blake said: they were first imagined, and not merely thought. Thought has tools to bend its objects, power to de-structure and modify them according to laws that we, more or less, know or believe we know. They are largely under the discretion of our will. Not so in the imagination: there, things that exist have some degree of autonomy and, at times, it is us who may be subject to their will.

"What is now proved was once only imagined": for this aphorism to be valid for that thing that is not a thing, in that part of the machine that is not a machine, that we call software, we need certain conditions. Because this purely imagined thing doesn't exist in the imagination of a single man but rather is distributed in the imagination of our two actors, as we have already clarified, purely for convenience: each one of them can represent several people. All the art (or science) of programming, all the designed tools we talked about: annotation systems, diagramming techniques, methodologies, are nothing but more or less imperfect languages to communicate these two imaginary worlds.

COMMENTS

According to Méher Baba, it's not necessary to have a complete map of the way to start the journey in the spiritual life. On the contrary, the insistence on having such full knowledge can hinder rather than help to advance. He who, from the shore speculates on the ocean, will know only its surface, but he who wants to know the depths must be willing to submerge.

from: Música Transpersonal, from Carlos D. Fregtman, Kairós editorials, Barcelona, 1990, pg. 206

0 1 1 0 1. YOU HAVE THE RIGHT TO BE LAZY

Orderly work has two faces: it works when our mind is clear. When it is full of confusing thoughts; discard them and do nothing: you have the right to be lazy.

EXPLANATION

There are some well-known stories of the great discoveries of science. Hamilton discovered that not all mathematical structures possess the commutative property while walking with his girlfriend through the countryside (it is said that he wrote A * B <> B * A on the stone of a bridge near where he had this insight). The walks of Einstein and Heisenberg, and other great thinkers are part of the mythology that surrounds these geniuses, and whether they are true or not, the important thing is that they make us think of a widespread phenomenon, which has many contradictory explanations, but that we all experiences at a certain moment: when you stop thinking about a problem, somehow 'your unconscious mind' (whatever that means), apparently continues working on it and, when you least expect it (even in dreams) the solution comes to you, unequivocally, clear like a vision.

COMMENTS

The poet Allen Ginsberg expressed the idea that creativity and meditation are inseparably linked, with the expression 'first thought / best thought.' This means that if you observe what happens in the flow of your consciousness with precision, vivid images will arise without effort and creating will seem more like transcribing.

Dimitri Ehrlich, Inside the Music, Shambala 1997, pg XI

0 1 1 1 0. THE TEMPORARY AND THE DEFINITIVE

Nothing is more definitive than the temporary. Think very carefully when you decide to place a fragment of temporary code, because it may end up being an unexpected and happy solution, or a problematic source of future problems.

EXPLANATION

Generally, the programmer is out of time and budget. Why? A vast literature on the management of projects, as well as the psychology of programming, accounts for this situation: what one thinks is not necessarily what one ends up doing. Systems respond to changing environments, the muse doesn't come when you call for her, but when she bloody wants to. One of the most common shortcuts we find to deliver a product is to establish routines or procedures created without much analysis, aware that they don't fully comply with what is required. We do this not because of irresponsibility, but because this small subroutine is necessary to conclude something more important, something that has to work. Time passes, we forget those temporary pieces and, eventually, they become an essential part of the final product.

COMMENTS

At about three or four hundred meters
of the Pyramid I bent down, took a handful
of sand, and dropped it silently a little
further and I said in a low voice: I'm modifying
the Sahara. The act was minimal, but the simple
words were accurate and I thought
all my life had been necessary for me to
say them. The memory of that moment is
one of the most significant of my stay in Egypt.

The desert – Jorge Luis Borges

0 1 1 1 1. DISCIPLINE

Discipline is a coercive force that is only morally acceptable when it arises from one's convictions and intense voluntary work based on our internal springs. Only strict discipline can guide the programmer in his arduous task and lead him to the conclusion of his Work. Concretely, discipline means a rigorous schedule of work, with carefully distributed moments of rest and generous distraction.

EXPLANATION

Discipline, order, efficiency, punctuality, are all terms that belong to the symbolic universe of our industrial society, the society of the machine. What is 'discipline' if not the correct functioning of a device? Externally imposed discipline turns men into machines, degrades and humiliates them, and with men like that, you can only have a world like the one we have. But when discipline and order are not imposed as a factor of production of wealth but are part of our spiritual attributes, when punctuality and administration of our work are the product of our internal development, these become the best tool for an artisan. And please, do not be confused! I'm not referring to 'internalized' industrial discipline; that is the worst kind. It makes people more into slaves than those who obey because they have no choice. With discipline, you can acquire knowledge; you can finish projects on time; you can enjoy the break you deserve. Vast knowledge doesn't guarantee excellent programming. Solid discipline allows us to acquire the knowledge to achieve it.

COMMENTS

"Craft follows tradition; discipline maintains the tradition."

Robert Fripp, Aphorisms

1 0 0 0 0. START OVER

To start over is always hard because it represents a failure, a false beginning, an incomplete or incorrect initial understanding that took us into a dead end. But there are situations where it's the only way out. Delete the file and start over.

EXPLANATION

Our culture, inherited from the Greeks, has a terrible myth: the story of Sisyphus. He was sentenced by the gods to push a rock up the top of a mountain which falls back each time, forcing him to start over for eternity. Many times programming complex routines or items we don't understand too well feel a lot like Sisyphus' punishment: we wasted hours of programming only to find out we were initially wrong and have to start from scratch. Sometimes, it seems to us that this situation can become permanent, in infinite. Our difference with this poor tragic hero is that we can 'give a twist' to our understanding of the problem and start again in earnest: that is, to rethink the problem in its entirety and not only in the fraction that causes the bother.

Starting from zero might be much more than just the solution to a routine that doesn't work, it can mean starting the whole program from scratch with a different vision, preferably after taking a break from work, reading a book, smoking a cigarette, or any pleasant activity. In other words: we can try, like Sisyphus, to push the rock up again, aware of the uselessness of our effort or we can (which the imaginary Greek couldn't) give ourselves a 'clean slate,' not to face the gods that rule the world of seemingly living machines and, with humility, erase everything and start over.

Starting over doesn't have to be a curse. Some have found in the process of repetition a comforting activity. In the north of Argentina, there is a town that happily rebuilds a bridge every year, destroyed every time again by heavy rains. On one occasion, the local authorities, thinking that they were doing good to their community, built a bridge according to the rules of proper engineering, which would resist the worst of the storms. This new bridge caused severe protests from the inhabitants of the region, who complained that the government had deprived them of one of the activities that defined their identity. The government understood the situation, destroyed the 'well made' bridge and the villagers continued with their 'primitive' bridge, rebuilding it at the end of each storm, exercising an activity whose sole purpose is itself. 'Starting from scratch' isn't always a punishment. Sometimes, it defines the character and meaning of a praxis.

COMMENTS

Some people have a hard time expressing themselves in their environment. This could be because they're avoiding self-expression, but it can
also be an indication that their means of expression are their clothes or
creative work, such as cooking or gardening. Others spend their time
planning and decorating their home, rearranging and changing the fur-
niture or creating endless 'do it yourself' projects to improve the house.

'House as a mirror of self', from Clare Cooper Marcus, Conari Press,
1995

1 0 0 0 1. DISTRACTIONS

The devil visits the monks to distract them from their meditations. Your mind is a swarm of ideas and ghosts that you must learn to tame.

EXPLANATION

In Christian literature, there is a great deal of reference, anecdote, and advice to fight off the demons that distract the faithful from his duties (especially in the Catholic religion, although there are some extraordinary passages from Luther on this as well). In the old Christian monasteries, a whole corpus of recommendations and exercises was developed to scare the Evil One away and frustrate his intentions. In Buddhism, there's an immense collection of texts intended to 'guide the mind', to dispel the thoughts that distract the concentration that will eventually lead to nirvana or culmination of the monk's work. That such distant religions from one another have been concerned, in different times, using absolutely different language and concepts, with the problem of thoughts that interfere with concentration, a concern taken up by both the New Age religions, as well as the investigations of psychology, gives testimony of the universal nature of this phenomenon. In the Chinese classic Monkey, which tells the adventures of a Buddhist monk who travels west in search of ancient manuscripts, the monkey represents thought, always jumping from one side to another and making mischief. Call it a monkey or a demon, autonomic dynamics of thought or simply distractions; you must learn to tame your mind. Distractions and boredom are responsible for a considerable part of the delays in projects and the involuntary production of errors in coding.

COMMENTS

"When the mind is silent, when it no longer projects itself inordinately into the future, wanting something, when the mind is genuinely serene, it becomes a mirror of the universe and the unknown manifests itself. You don't have to look for it; you can't attract it. You can only attract that which you know. You can not invite an unknown guest, but you can have faith in his existence. You can only invite people you know.

The new can bear fruit when the field is ready, when the soil is tilled. But remember, you can't quiet down the lake; it only quiets down when the breeze stops."

Música Transpersonal, Carlos D. Fregtman. pg. 207

1 0 0 1 0. YOU'RE EACH TIME FURTHER AWAY

The fact that the program is finished from the point of view of the client doesn't mean that it is finished from your point of view.

EXPLANATION

There is something paradoxical in the pursuit of a goal; building an artifact, like a program, finding the solution to a problem or composing a poem: each step presents us with dilemmas and each possible path that we consider branches into alternatives, in a recursive form, ad infinitum. To create means knowing which option to discard, which suggestions to ignore.

COMMENTS

In the Book of the 24 Philosophers, it reads: 'God: love that hides ever more in the same measure it is owned.'

1 0 0 1 1. YOUR WORLD DOESN'T BELONG TO YOU

Each program is a small world of which you are the creating god, the demiurge. In that world you are almighty: you possess all its secrets, you know all its ways. Remember that for every world created by a god, there is a devil that messes it all around. Take care of your world, the garden where you lodged your favorite creatures, do not lose sight of the small or the big. Your world doesn't belong to you, but you are responsible for it.

EXPLANATION

In Gnostic theology, the demiurge is a lower and imperfect god, and the world he creates is full of errors, precisely because of the imperfection of its creator. Far from the kind and all-knowing god of Christianity and other monotheistic religions, the Gnostic demiurge is clumsy and incapable of putting order in his creation.

The art of programming tends to create in the practitioner a false sense of security, which leads him to trust his abilities and his intuitions, often at the expense of careful and meticulous testing. As the demiurge of heretics, we are sometimes clumsy and victims of our skills.

COMMENTS

Can God play a significant game with his own creature? Can any creator, even a limited one, play a significant game with his own creature?

1 0 1 0 0. IRRESPONSIBILITY

Do not confuse your right to laziness and the natural obstacles of your trade with a license to forget the discipline which defines you as a programmer.

EXPLANATION

Distinguishing between the necessary autonomous administration of time, and the demands of the client that provides your sustenance are essential to be able to exercise your trade with effectiveness and satisfaction. The unpredictability of the 'sparks' of creation, the difficulties that this strange machine, that is almost not a machine, presents to us, and the dance of imaginary demons that in a moment overwhelm you, can lead you to an undeserved inactivity, to the unfulfillment of your contractual duties, and eventually, to the loss of reputation or work.

COMMENTS

An error is always forgivable, rarely excusable and always unacceptable.

Robert Fripp, Aphorisms

1 0 1 0 1. INEXPRESSIBLE

Not all ideas or feelings are expressible in words. Not all the needs of the client or user can be automated according to their particular vision. For the ideas that can't be put into words, we have gestures, music, or silence. For the functions that can't be programmed, we should recommend a change of platform, language, or simply an efficient way to perform these tasks manually.

EXPLANATION

That a whole dimension of human existence is alien to symbolization, to language, may seem to us like one of many paradoxes that philosophers like to invent, until the time comes when we have to express feelings or explain situations for which we literally have no words. In some cases, it's simply because of circumstance (a condition of seriousness, strong emotions) and in many others, merely a lack of ability to use all the possibilities of the language. Not everyone has the pen of Proust or Balzac, nor can draw like Picasso, nor write programs like Donald Knuth.

But there are other times, perhaps rarer, less frequent for most people when you just can not express that fragment of the real world that affects you. There is an inherent flaw in the human language and in all our symbolic systems that does not allow us to express all the truths that compose the universe covered by that symbolic system.

Mystics of all times have talked about' that which can not be named', implying that when we try to put into words the source of all existence, we necessarily falsify the reality of that source, which is not susceptible to be apprehended by words or thought. In Christianity, the so-called 'negative theology' makes similar claims about God, a being of whom nothing can be said up, for we would be talking of something else.

A computer program is a system of symbols, with certain peculiar characteristics but, in short, most definitely a system of symbols. It's reasonable to expect that some 'truths' of the universe that you're responsible for, that is, some operations performed by men in the real world, are not susceptible to automatization through a specific programming tool.

COMMENTS

The Tao that can be told is not the true Tao.

Lao-Tze, Tao Te Ching

1 0 1 1 0. YESTERDAY IT WORKED FINE

Programs stop working, the same way people get sick or plants wither.

EXPLANATION

There is a popular saying: 'for something to be damaged, all it takes is for it to be working well first'. No doubt there are causes for a program to stop running totally or partially: a modification in a module that, without anyone realizing it, had an impact on another apparently unrelated module, an error in the hardware, a condition in the environment (the network, the electrical wiring, the atmospheric conditions, the changes users make to the parameters of their work station, an error in another program that affects ours, among other possibilities) could be the unknown responsible of 'yesterday everything worked fine, and today it doesn't'. There are different strategies for this situation, most of the time it is: merely doing nothing. If the cause lies within one of these environmental factors, they will go as they came, long before our technical skills help us find the root of the problem. This, however, should not be an excuse for not thinking about possible causes and trying to experiment with different hypotheses. It's the obligation of the programmer to think about all reasonable options. But you shouldn't forget that, often, given the complexity of current systems and your inevitable partial and fragmented knowledge of all the variables involved, the best thing to do is simply to wait. Or, as the famous joke says, turn off the computer and turn it on again.

COMMENTS

If you were driving your car and suddenly it stopped, would you think that it suffered a breakdown, or would you say: "wait a moment, it can't be broken, yesterday it was working fine"?

If you were watching TV and the screen went completely black, would you think that it was damaged, or would you believe that that's impossible since it had never happened before?

If you see a sign warning that the highway is flooded, would you think that this may not be true since yesterday it wasn't?

These questions are always present in my heart, since what I hear most about computers is "how can it be damaged or why doesn't it work properly if until yesterday it was going perfectly?"

Found in a discussion forum on the Internet moderated by Shaun,
March 3rd, 1999

1 0 1 1 1. THE PROGRAM KEEPS ON RUNNING IN YOUR HEAD

Your brain, in a very limited and metaphoric way, continues executing the program when you turn off the computer.

EXPLANATION

Although any similarity between the human brain and the computer is only a remnant of the science fiction of the 1950'ies and the mechanistic or reductionist visions promoted by the schools of psychology, it's only a metaphor at best. But this unhappy metaphor serves to describe a phenomenon very common to programmers: the obsessive thoughts that arise in the mind of the craftsman when he is at home or walking down the street. It seems that the program is still running in his head, and in his head, he discovers errors or new possibilities.

COMMENTS

Frederick Brooks, jr., writes in The Mythical Man – Month:

The programmer, like the poet, works only slightly removed from pure thought-stuff. He builds his castles in the air, from air, creating by exertion of the imagination. Few media of creation are so flexible, so easy to polish and rework, so readily capable of realizing grand conceptual structures.

1 1 0 0 0. THE BLIND SPOT

There's something within your program that you can not see: it is right between your eyes, at that point where the gaze fails, called 'the blind spot'. Just by changing the position in your mind, you might be able to see it.

EXPLANATION

To understand something, nothing like examining the obvious, that which we take for granted, and see if it's indeed as obvious as we're used to thinking.

Many times the obvious is such because the eye sees only one part or aspect of it, which happens to be compatible with something we know. But usually, if we examine it from another angle, or if we carry certain analogies to their extremes, certain similarities to their limit, the absurd appears, the contradiction. The obvious was not obvious at all.

Let's start with certain basic notions the way common sense treats them. We're not interested in formal definitions, because even those who create them, only operate with them in limited points of their thinking, not in the continuum of real life. A physicist may know that an object is 99% empty space, but still, he sits in an unreal chair and eats on an unreal table.

It is the notions of common sense that guide our unconscious premises, and they are, therefore, the ones that can be an obstacle to our understanding. Formal notions have gone through the purification of reason, and in general (or so we like to believe) we understand their implications.

Well, is there something more obvious than a machine, a user, a program? Here, in the obvious, might be our blind spot: in what we don't question, in what we take for granted.

1 1 0 0 1. WORLDS WITHIN WORLDS

*Your program is an imperfect, incomplete, and defor-
med reflection of a portion of the world. Each routine of your
program is an imperfect, incomplete, and deformed reflection
of your program — each routine within a routine.*

EXPLANATION

Seen from outer space, as satellite photographs show us, the earth is a
beautiful sphere covered with blue seas and brown continents, perfectly
delineated. It looks like those maps in school, whose sharp contours we
laboriously learned to repeat to be able to reproduce them in the geo-
graphy exams. The truth is that, if the camera of our satellite zooms in,
the perfectly regular coasts become intricate curves with ins and outs.
The closer we get, we find levels of detail so tiny that they don't even
have a name. They are not bays or fjords anymore; they are simply ir-
regularities like those we encounter in a walk along any beach. When
our 'zoom' touches the earth, the curve, the border, the line that from a

distance drew an identifiable coastline, has vanished. We find rocks and fragments of territory completely incapable of constituting a demarcation only perceptible from afar. It is what's called the 'fractal nature' of our world. Fractals are mathematical structures characterized by containing, within each of their parts, fragments or whole copies of the whole, recursively and infinitely.

The idea that the world (or parts of it) is made up of copies of the whole, and these copies, in turn, share the same structure, has been intuited from the most distant times. The oriental carpets, the intricate designs of the Baroque, the recursive structure of Bach's fugues announced the discoveries of Mandelbrot, the father of fractal geometry. A computer program, given that it is is a formal symbolic construct is impregnated with recursive structures, whether the programmer who built it knows it or not. I'm not just referring to the explicit use of recursive functions (that is, fragments of code that invoke themselves). There is something deeply recursive in the fact that we write our software in a language, which works thanks to a compiler, which is written in a language, which...

COMMENTS

The protean nature of the computer is such that it can act like a machine or like a language to be shaped and exploited. It is a medium that can dynamically simulate the details of any other medium, including media that cannot exist physically. It is not a tool, although it can act like many tools. It is the first meta medium, and as such it has degrees of freedom for representation and expression never before encountered and as yet barely investigated. Even more important, it is fun and therefore intrinsically worth doing.

Alan Kay, 'Computer Software', Scientific American, September 1984

1 1 0 1 0. OBJECTS WITHOUT OBJECTS

Don't be afraid to cut out entire portions of your code if
you discover they don't do anything.

EXPLANATION

During the construction of a program, we develop routines, structures, objects, procedures, whose degree of relevance changes as the project evolves. A considerable part of the code of a system can be made of segments that are never executed since they were written in stages of lower development of the project and never erased. Any programmer has witnessed the disconcerting spectacle of eliminating dozens or even hundreds of lines of code, only to discover the program runs just fine. The proliferation of useless code does not necessarily reflect professional ineptitude from the craftsman (although yes, this factor may be present). It's more like those 'dead ends' that any project in which we're required to rehearse several possible scenarios is a victim of: attempted solutions that are first drafted and then abandoned or forgotten because, although they do nothing, they do not bother or do not let themselves be noticed.

We mustn't show any mercy on these fragments of code, even if we developed a sentimental attachment to them, or if they constitute an in-surmountable sample of our skills as craftsmen (you can back them up if you want to keep these samples of your art). But they must be rooted out like cancer!

1 1 0 1 1. CLOSE YOUR EYES AND TRY TO SEE

Inner vision many times shows us the world with greater clarity and sharpness than our eyes.

EXPLANATION

Closing your eyes to see seems like an impractical recommendation since it is precisely the eyes that give us the sense of sight. But 'seeing' does not only mean perceiving external reality. We also 'see' our memories, our problems, or their solutions, our future. Seeing in this sense is partly to imagine, to summon images and to examine them with an eye that is also imaginary but not less acute. We can not think without phantoms, wrote Aristotle, and by phantoms he meant the images that our mind generates spontaneously at times, intentionally when we work on it. By closing the eyes and letting the mind wander, the 'phantoms' or images spontaneously produced by our brain acquire different configurations, not unlike the shapes in a kaleidoscope. In certain very special moments, when the petals of our sensitivity are open, and our thoughts rest in the soft calm of a lake where there is no breeze to shake its waters, it is possible to see in those images fragments of ideas, concepts, messages that come from within us and whose recipient we are ourselves. It is possible, as it happens in dreams, or during sudden bursts of imagination that we find ourselves thinking of any random thing and as if by magic, we see what we were looking for right before our eyes.

COMMENTS

The measure of Kepler's genius is offered by the intensity of his contradictions and the use he made of them. We have seen him walk laboriously, with infinite patience, along monotonous trial and error, and then suddenly lift the flight when a fortunate assumption or chance offered him an auspicious occasion. What allowed him to instantly recognize his possibilities when the number 0.00429 appeared in an unexpected context was the fact that both his deserted mind and his unconscious sleepwalking were saturated with all the conceivable aspects of his problem, not only with the numerical data and the relationships but also with an intuitive *sensation* of the physical powers and the *gestalt* configurations that they implied. A locksmith who opens a complicated lock with a rough piece of bent wire is not guided by logic but by the unconscious residue of innumerable past experiences that confer on his touch a pearl of wisdom that his reason does not possess.

Arthur Koestler, Kepler, 1985

1 1 1 0 0. FALSE SOLUTIONS

*Don't fall in love with your creations to the point where
they close the road for you to reach your goals (don't be
afraid to lose them: they will always come back to you because they came out of your spirit).*

EXPLANATION

We know that our mind is easy prey to illusions. If we find ourselves lost
in a dense forest at night or incapable of finding a way out of a boiling desert, fear can get the best of us. In such extreme situations, mirages and
illusions are common phenomena. By the way, the word illusion comes
from the Latin ludere, a verb which means 'to play'. Our mind plays with
us in certain circumstances. The stress produced by a project whose
deadline is expired, or a subroutine that doesn't work as desired despite
all the analyzes of our colleagues, can also constitute situations such
as the dark forest or the desert. The mind can, in those moments, play
tricks on us, and convince us that the solution is in our hands, and this

can be one of the hardest convictions to defeat. When the mind comes up with an answer, driven by despair, it covers it with an aura of certainty that makes us waste a lot of time trying to understand why it does not work if 'it really is the solution' and it often prevents us from even asking ourselves if it is the result of a rational analysis or a wrong intuition.

False solutions can be one of the worst enemies of the programmer, and one should always be on guard against them. There are no recipes to avoid them. Only that 'old gentleman behind closed doors called common sense', as the great Engels once said, can from time to time, if we let him, come to our aid.

COMMENTS

The adaptation of machinery can only be perfected by him who, as it were, enters into it, making it an incarnation of himself, an enlargement of his own organism. Oliver Wendell Holmes has described this putting of his life into a rowing boat – his every volition extending as perfectly into his oars as if his spinal column ran down the center of the keel. So the thoughtful locomotive driver is clothed with all the attributes of a power superior to his own, except volition. Every faculty is stimulated and every sense exalted.

Alexander Holley, The Uncertain Relation between Science, Engineering and Art, 1876 in: Elting Morison, The Uncertain Relation, Dae-
dalus, Vol. 109, No. 1, Modern Technology: Problem or Opportunity?
(Winter, 1980), pp. 179-184

1 1 1 0 1. THE SIMPLEST SOLUTION

Everything should be made as simple as possible, but not simpler. (Albert Einstein)

EXPLANATION

It is paradoxical that a text that preaches the complex nature of computer systems and that insists on pointing out the frequent mistake of thinking complexity through simplicity (the sentence is by Edgar Morin), also proposes the current aphorism, that 'the best solution is the simplest one'.

The paradox and the contradiction it implies are only apparent. The complex nature of computer systems is one of the many obstacles to its build-up and maintenance and eventually to its understanding. The relationship between the physical part (the hardware), the different layers of the operating systems, the interface, the programming languages and other components of the software, and finally the user, constitute a complex structure. The programming of such a structure so that it performs a set of useful operations, even when it must take into account the complexity of the system, must seek maximum simplicity in its construction. Simplicity doesn't mean avoiding the complex, but rather it englobes the 'clear', the pleasant and the practical. It is a bit of a delicate quality to define.

An illustration of this can be found in the poetry of some great masters, such as Antonio Machado: in plain words and working within traditional poetic structures, that is to say, in a 'simple' way, he managed to capture deep and immensely complex feelings, which can only be said the way he said them, or else one would have to build endless paraphrases in prose that would inevitably betray the clear and unfathomable meaning of his poems.

There was a sailor
who made a garden by the sea,
and who became a gardener.
Was the garden in bloom,
the gardener left, for those seas of God.

Simple lines of unparalleled beauty conceal an infinite of feelings and ideas. Machado was a great artisan of the language: he approached the complexity of the human soul with a maximum economy of words. With rhetorical figures, he uses the simplest solution to express the complex. There is no contradiction or paradox, or rather, the paradox lays somewhere else: it is in the nature of things to be complicated and at the same time to allow themselves to be described in simple terms. To arrive at those 'simple' terms, to reach that economy of means that the aphorism proposes, constitutes perhaps the most arduous work of a true artisan.

COMMENTS

We start, then, with nothing, pure zero. But this is not the nothing of negation. For not means other than, and other is merely a synonym of the ordinal numeral second. As such it implies a first; while the present pure zero is prior to every first. The nothing of negation is the nothing of death, which comes second to, or after, everything. But this pure zero is the nothing of not having been born. There is no individual thing, no compulsion, outward nor inward, no law. It is the germinal nothing, in which the whole universe is involved or foreshadowed. As such, it is absolutely undefined and unlimited possibility — boundless possibility. There is no compulsion and no law. It is boundless freedom.

Charles S. Peirce, Logic of Events, 1898

1 1 1 1 0. DON'T DO ANYTHING

*Stay silent, watch your screen flicker, or simply close
your eyes. Watch your thoughts go by as if they were clouds
but do not stop on any of them.*

EXPLANATION

There are times when our interaction with the computer is useless and can be harmful, as happens between people when a succession of verbal exchanges brings the dialogue to a standstill: anything we say will only make things worse.

The same can happen with our computer. After hours of unsuccessful struggle with a problem, we begin to make mistakes, to erase the wrong files, to damage what was correct. In those cases, it is better to suspend all activity, take some time, try to 'quiet down the waters of the mind', as the Buddhists say, literally 'do not think of anything'. That white canvas in which we turn our mind, if we manage to do it, will very soon begin to paint itself, to draw on its surface the figure that will untie the knots of our imagination and allow us to continue our Work.

COMMENTS

If you find the leading edge, you can do anything. If you knew all about it, it wouldn't be the leading edge.

Karl Pribram, quoted in 'Música Transpersonal', by Carlos D. Fregt-man, Editorial Kairós, Barcelona, 1990. (free translation by the editor)

1 1 1 1 1. THE MASTERPIECE

Aspire to perfection, but accept that perfection does not exclude error, but rather presupposes it.

EXPLANATION

Finally, we come to that character who is the ultimate reason for our work: the client. Many times, depending on how we work or how the company we work for is structured, we never meet the client personally. Sometimes we don't even know who it is, or he or she might be just an abstraction, like Project XXX, or the program for Company ZZZ. Other times, we interact directly with this character, who might not be a single person or a single department (perhaps a large corporation) but who communicates with us through persons. And although contractually the client is the Corporation YYY, for us, the client is that (or those) person(s) with whom we speak, to whom we deliver our products, with whom we discuss the problems.

Now, this client (let's take the simplest case and assume it's a single person) has an extraordinary mission that might seem strange or incredible, but we'll soon show its absolute rationality. The purpose of this client is to be dissatisfied with our services. He pays us not to understand his needs, and we accept the work knowing that we don't understand what he wants and that, even if we understand it, we can not satisfy him. Am I ironic, or worse yet, cynical? None of these: although irony and cynicism are two essential qualities for this trade.

Let's look more closely at the relationship between client and programmer. First of all, the client doesn't have any necessity to satisfy, at least not in the common understanding of the word 'necessity'. On the other hand, successfully communicating a necessity requires a series of verbal skills that clients usually do not possess, regardless of their education or intelligence. To express in words, the supposed necessity that an information system must satisfy exceeds the verbal abilities of any literate person. The client doesn't have technological requirements; the client has needs that have to do with his own business. Put yourself in his or her shoes. Suppose we go to a fancy restaurant for dinner. We're the 'client'; the cook is the 'programmer'. He'll prepare for us a 'product' to respond to our 'needs' (we can regard the maître as a systems analyst or an information engineer). We go to a restaurant for all sorts of reasons: we don't feel like cooking, there is no food in our house, or we simply want something different, perhaps we're holding a business meeting, or someone is getting married. Food as such (the 'product'), is only one element (and possibly not the most important) of our needs. But the maître, the waiter and the cook can only take care of that product, because that is what they sell, and in terms of that product we are customers, and they are programmers. The desired product (its 'specifications') are straightforward: they are stipulated in a menu. Sometimes, if you are a habitué of the place, you can ask for exceptions (a special sauce, a different way of preparing a dish), as long as the maître consults with the cook and this one has the required ingredients on hand. Otherwise, we're restricted to the menu. If we assume that these gentlemen working at the restaurant are intelligent, we won't have much problem communicating what we want to them. Worst case scenario, if we're unhappy, we don't return, and the matter ends there.

Let's look at our real programmers and customers. For starters, there isn't a menu with well-defined options. The exceptions made in the restaurant with select customers and the consent of the cook are the normal situation here. Communication between client and programmer is one of the toughest problems in the negotiation process.

There are vast differences between a restaurant and the creation of a program, but there are some similarities as well: in both cases, the needs that trigger the customer-provider relationship, are often secondary, and the product we deliver to the customer rarely has to do with technological elements or aspects of business procedures; as well as in the restaurant it may be more important what the pianist is playing than the salmon sauce we're being served.

Let's play with some axioms.

The client is a creature who will always be dissatisfied with our services because the relationship we usually establish with him is destined to produce such dissatisfaction.

The client pays us to deliver a product that does not correspond to his real needs, and no methodology in the world can free us from this paradox.

If I am allowed one last analogy, I'd like to refer back to the craftsmen of the Middle Ages. Those corporations of blacksmiths, stone carvers, carpenters, who built the Gothic cathedrals: what needs did their products fulfill? Not any that the 'clients' (the whole town) could express in words. These artisans worked to build a mystery, a work that brought them closer to God, that gave meaning to their community, and they did it without knowing they were doing it. Humbly, for decades, even centuries, passing their work from fathers to sons, they built those marvels. The people were happy and proud, a need was fulfilled, although nobody ever wrote it down or possibly conceived it in his mind.

Gothic cathedrals are full of asymmetries, design errors, incongruous mixtures of stylistic elements (the Paris cathedral is adorned with Egyptian statues of the goddess Isis, in a false representation of the Virgin Mary). It is this set of defects, of errors, of mistakes that time has diluted, through the ignorance of those who contemplate them. It's that incomplete, rustic, incoherent character, which makes them perfect and insurmountable creations.

When programming is successful, when the client is satisfied, when we manage to break the vicious circle of paradoxes that I referred to earlier, it's because we managed to establish a human connection with the client, we managed to penetrate (many times without realizing it) into what's essential for him, we manage to establish a communication that goes beyond the diagrams, the sessions of 'brainstorming' and the documents of service proposals, which are all ways of avoiding a human encounter. All these documents constitute that perverse (but necessary) use of language that ultimately prevents their real exercise. If we achieve that communication, if we can understand our client humanly, if he is able, in turn, to understand our limitations (time, knowledge, technology, budgets, and also human, personal circumstances, in short: our world), then we will have achieved our goal: to be excellent craftsmen and to complete the Masterpiece.

www.ingramcontent.com/pod-product-compliance
Lightning Source LLC
Chambersburg PA
CBHW021436210526
45463CB00002B/533